STECK-[illegible]
NEW WAY
HEADS and TAILS

Pigs

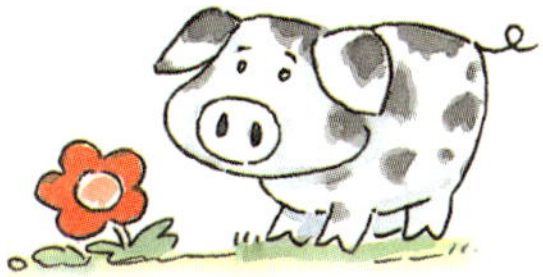

STECK-VAUGHN COMPANY
A Division of Harcourt Brace & Company

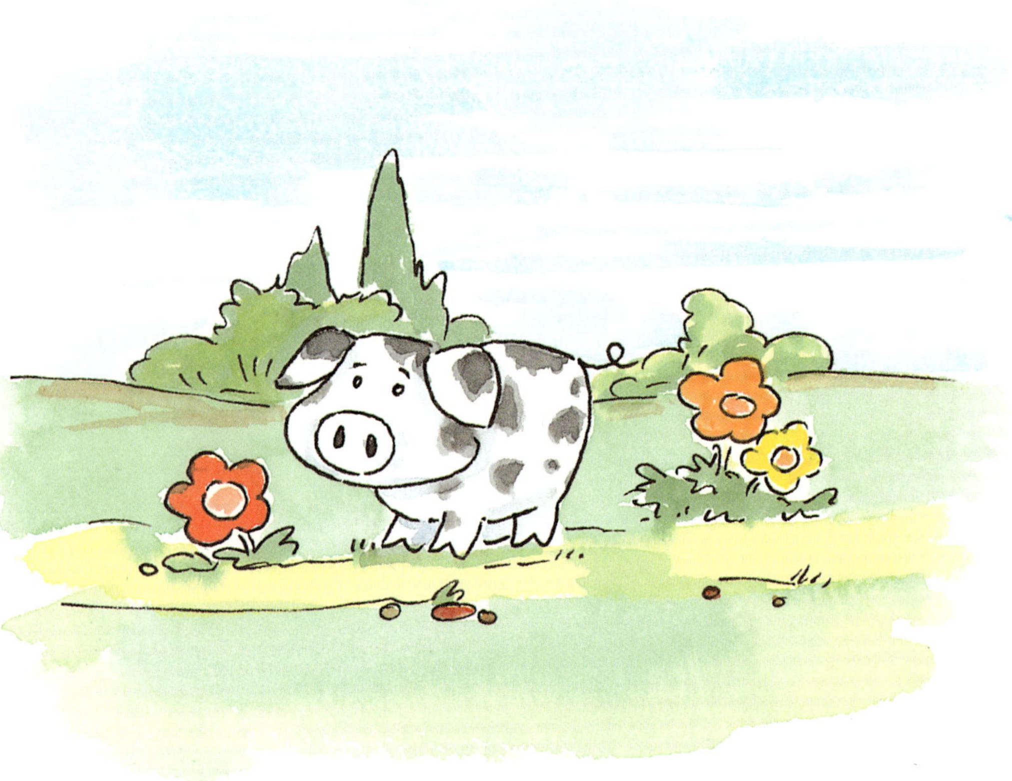

a small pig

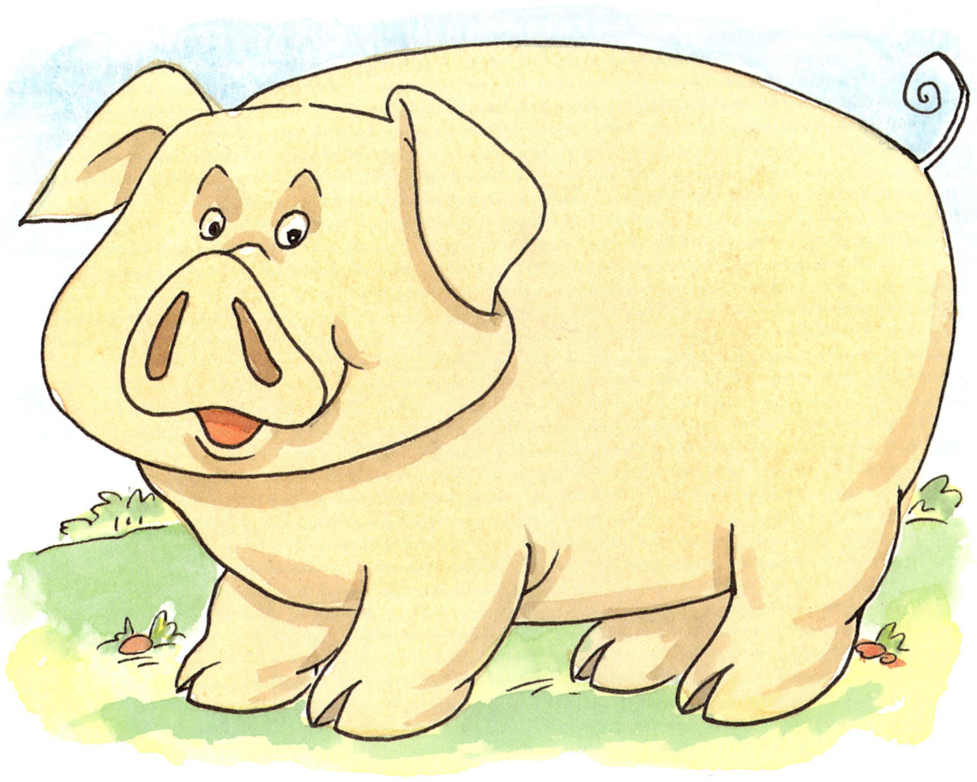

a big pig

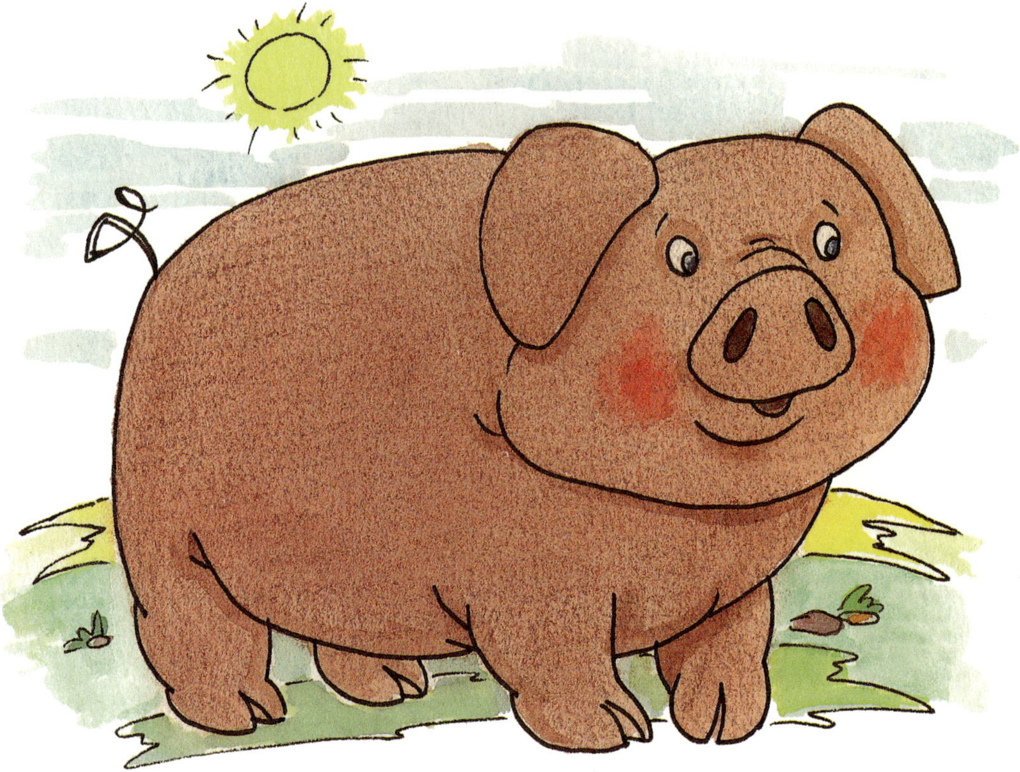

a brown pig

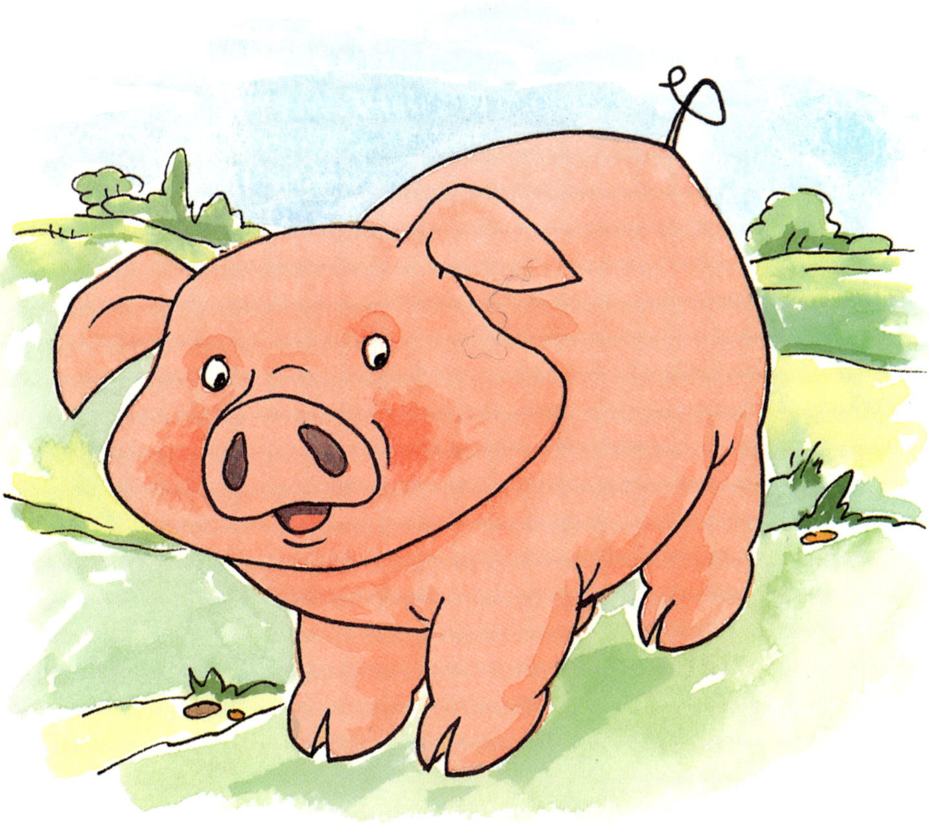

a pink pig

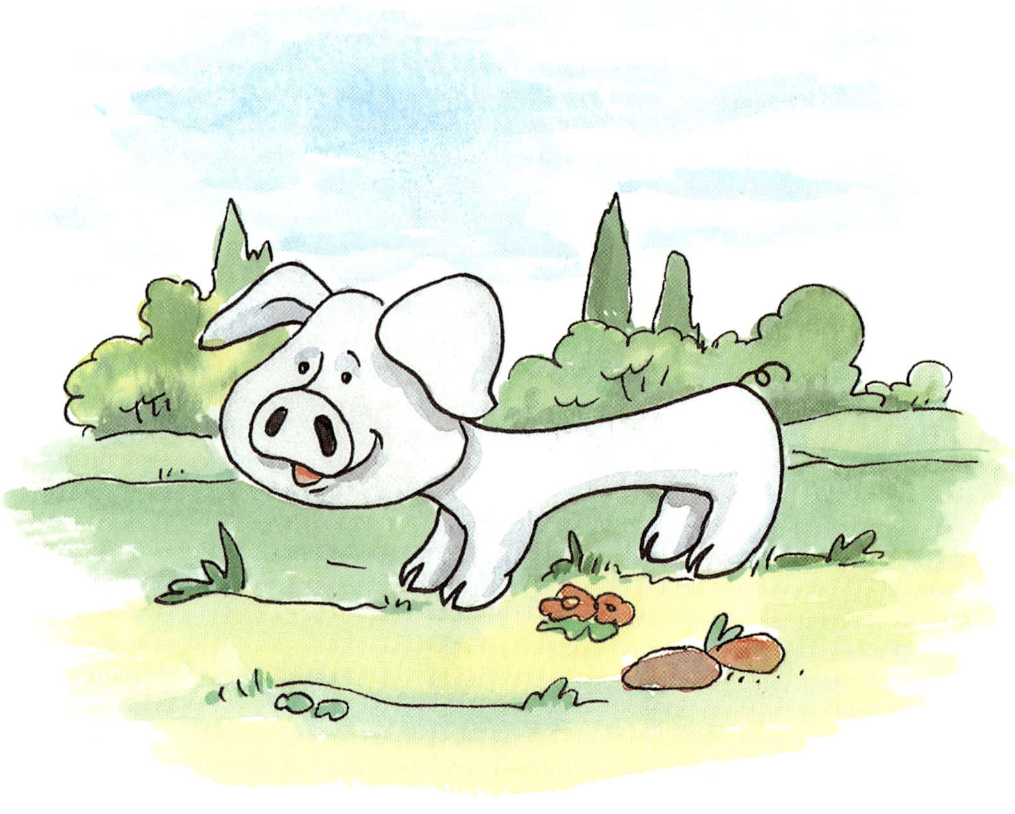

a short pig

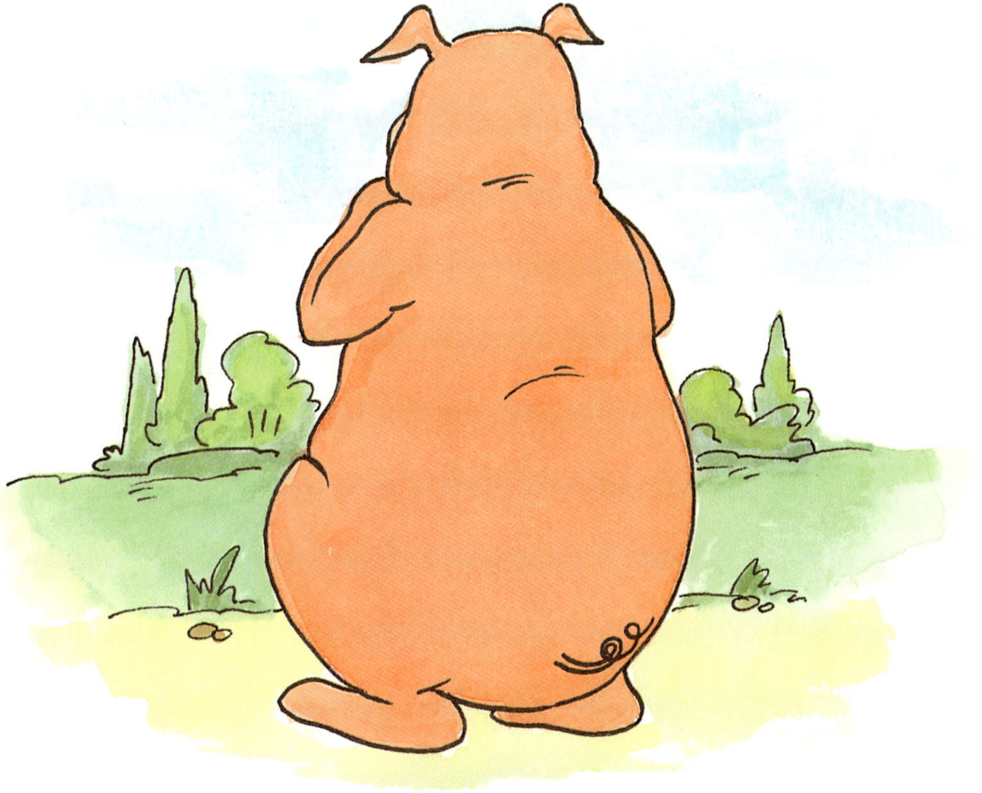

a tall pig

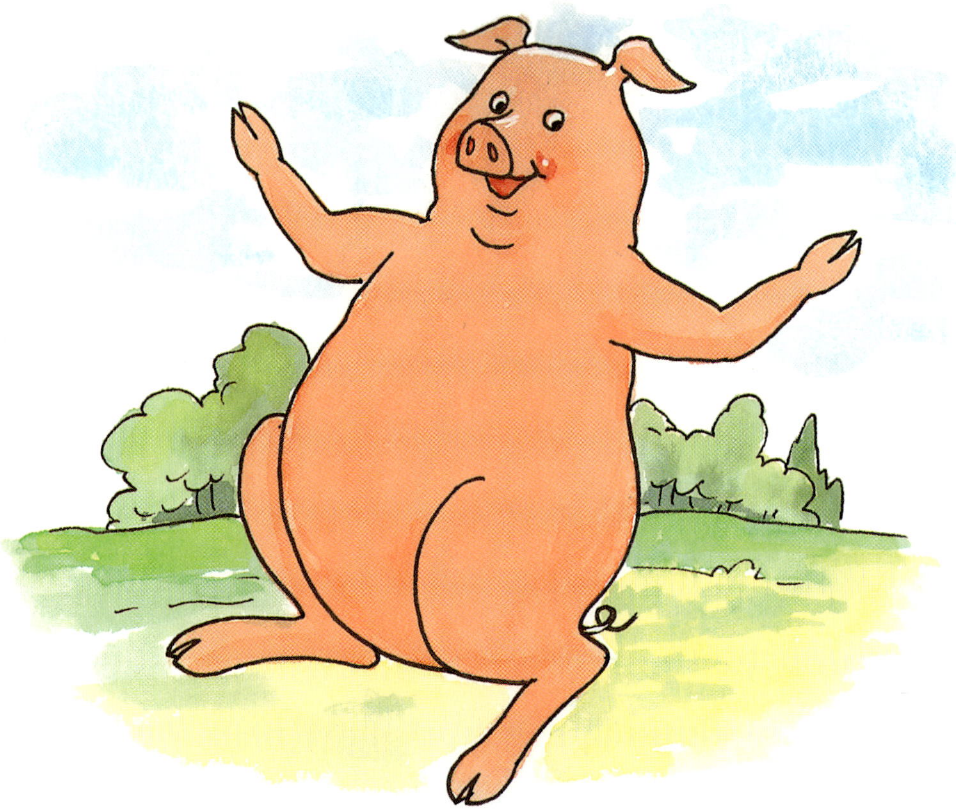

Tom pig!